Debbie
learns to dance

GILBERT DELAHAYE - MARCEL MARLIER

AWARD PUBLICATIONS — LONDON

The author and publisher acknowledge with thanks
the advice and collaboration of Madame Dolores Laga,
professor of dancing at the *Theatre Royal de la Monnaie*
and soloist with the *Ballet Bejart*
and of Miss Nesta Brooking, principal of the
Studio of Ballet and General Education in
the preparation of this book.

"Mummy, may I go to ballet classes?" asked
Debbie, who had been to see the ballet *Cinderella*
for her Christmas treat. "I want to be a
ballerina!"

"You can't turn into a ballerina overnight,"
laughed her mother. "And only one person in
a thousand has the right kind of talent."

Debbie thought for a moment and then said:

"Really what I want is not just to be a ballerina
but to learn to be a good dancer. Do you think
I could do that?"

"It would mean a lot of very hard work."

"Please may I try?"

Mademoiselle Irene, the dancing teacher, was very patient with her new pupil.

"Turn your leg out, Debbie. Keep your arms rounded like this, look... that's much better."

As mother said, "Before you can be a dancer you have to practise and practise and make yourself supple right to the tips of your fingers."

Mademoiselle Irene had to explain over and over again to Debbie how to move her feet outwards and raise her arms without stiffening up, but keeping perfectly natural and relaxed.

"Now, Debbie, a dancer must know how to do these five positions correctly, but that isn't all. A dancer is useless if she can't bend her knees smoothly and rise up on her toes. It isn't very easy."

1st position

2nd position

3rd position

4th position

5th position

Below : 1. demi-plié. – 2. plié. – 3. relevé sur demi-pointes.

① ② ③

So, before she could begin to be a good pupil, Debbie had to repeat over and over again steps like the *dégagé,* the *grand battement* and the *rond de jambe.*

Above :
1. dégagé in 2nd –
2. dégagé in 4th de-
vant. – 3. dégagé der-
rière croisé.

left :
grand battement
below :
rond de jambe

"Oh, no! Not carelessly, like that! Do it as well as you possibly can. Don't wobble! It is only by persevering that you will ever learn to be a useful dancer."

"Come along, girls; once again, please. Watch yourselves in the mirror at the end of the room and follow the beat! One... two... three... four... All together, please. You must get this one better before we go on to the next exercise."

"Debbie, I should like you to demonstrate an *attitude,*" said the teacher. Debbie concentrated hard and remembered all the things she had been told.

"Well done, dear, that was very nice. You are really trying hard and coming along well. I am very pleased with you."

Debbie tried not to look too self-satisfied!

attitude de dos à la barre

It was very hard work at the ballet school! Every day there were new exercises to be learned. Debbie had to bend backwards, first of all holding on to the barre to help her keep her balance, and later on without any support. She had to learn to stretch her leg up straight, holding on to her heel to keep steady.

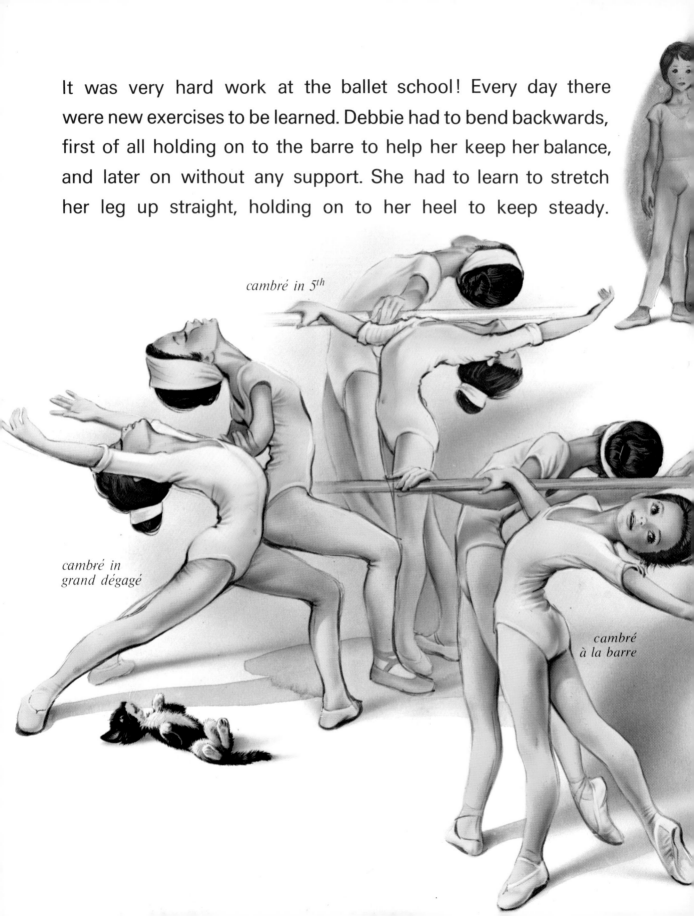

cambré in 5th

cambré in
grand dégagé

cambré
à la barre

Some of the bigger girls could stretch even better than she could, but sometimes she thought that Mademoiselle Irene's little cat did his exercises better than anybody, without any practice at all. As the days became weeks, the teacher could see that Debbie had both talent and perseverance.

exercices d'assouplissement

pied à la main

grand battement
en attitude

Debbie began to think about the future. She knew now what it meant to be a dancer and that was what she really wanted to be more than anything in the world. She wondered how well she would do in the examinations that she would soon have to take. The best pupils were sometimes accepted for the big ballet school attached to the Opera House, and this was her greatest ambition. But it all depended on the examination results, and on whether the doctors thought she had the right physique for a dancer. Dancers must not be too tall and they must be very strong, because dancing is such hard work.

port de bras en grand écart

There is much more to dancing than just being able to perform the difficult steps. Debbie had to learn how to move her arms smoothly and gracefully, bending down as if to pick a flower, or raising her hands to her head, like a queen putting on her crown. In a ballet, every tiny movement is important and means something. A dancer must be as supple as a cat, as light as a feather, as agile as a squirrel and as graceful and dignified as a swan!

dégagé in 4th
pointe derrière
bras en couronne

mouvement d'adage

When Debbie was dancing, she had to imagine herself in all sorts of different parts. Sometimes she would be a firefly, darting to and fro over the grass; sometimes a butterfly, floating gently on the wind.

It takes more than one lesson to learn how to dance like that, but Debbie thought it was worth all the trouble and hard work!

*adage avec arabesque
penchée au milieu*

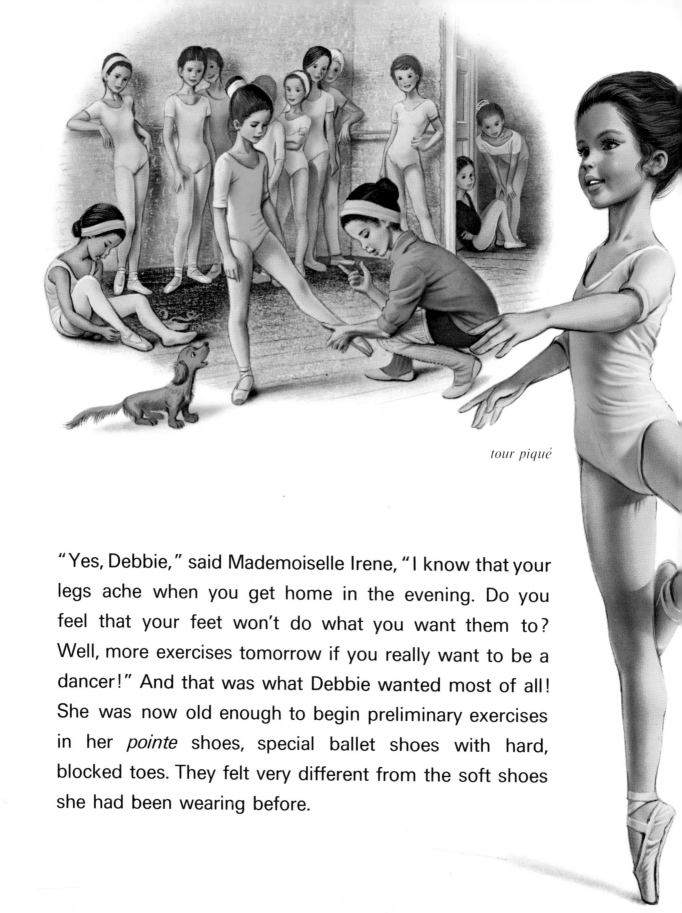

tour piqué

"Yes, Debbie," said Mademoiselle Irene, "I know that your legs ache when you get home in the evening. Do you feel that your feet won't do what you want them to? Well, more exercises tomorrow if you really want to be a dancer!" And that was what Debbie wanted most of all! She was now old enough to begin preliminary exercises in her *pointe* shoes, special ballet shoes with hard, blocked toes. They felt very different from the soft shoes she had been wearing before.

After many weeks of practice at last she was able to *bourrée* swiftly and lightly on her toes, which seemed to bring her joyously nearer to her aim of becoming a *real* dancer. As she practised, Debbie thought of the last time her mother and father had taken her to see a ballet, and how, when the lights in the great Opera House had dimmed, the curtain rose to show the stage, and the ballerina floating into the spotlight like a drifting feather.

piqué arabesque

entrechat quatre

glissade « saut de chat »

pas de bourrée

grand jeté en tournant

glissade grand jeté

ports de bras

But everybody in the dancing class cannot turn into a prima ballerina! Only people with outstanding talent can do that, and Debbie felt that if, by practice and hard work, she could become as good a dancer as it was possible for her to be, she would be happy. But she knew too, that she would never stop trying to get better!

Debbie had done well in her examinations, and at last, feeling rather nervous, she waited with the others for her audition and interview at the Opera Ballet School. To her delight, she was awarded a scholarship!

That night lying in bed, her thoughts were filled with dancing and as soon as she fell asleep she started to dream. She was light as a feather in the wind. Effortlessly she moved through *glissades, entrechats;* she soared high in a *grand jeté,* floated across the floor in a *pas de bourrée,* sprang, neat-footed in a *pas de chat.* She knew that all her movements were perfect, without any faults at all, light and easy! Perhaps this is how the birds feel, she thought, when the wind catches them and tosses them in the air.

Oh, this is a nice dream, I hope it goes on and on...

Now Debbie's dream was changing...

She was by herself in the middle of a great stage, red velvet curtains looped back on each side; and there, beyond the lights was the theatre, packed with people. She must dance her very best for them.

As she moved gracefully to the music of *Cinderella,* the ballet she had first seen and remembered so well, she knew she had never danced better in all her life. She was so immersed in the ballet that she did not even hear the twelve chimes of midnight as they struck...

Then suddenly everything was transformed! The stage blazed with light, the Prince leaped on and Debbie was a princess! He lifted her into the spotlight, and she balanced in his arms like a bird.

Oh, how lovely it was to dance!

It was a wonderful dream... and perhaps, if she goes on working and practising Debbie may become a ballerina one day. But whatever happens, she will go on working and practising, just the same, sometimes tired, even discouraged, but always sure that her chief ambition is... to dance!